3.75

DISCARDED FROM THE
PORTVILLE FREE LIBRARY

The FIRST BOOK of the
WAR OF 1812

For IRIS and ELLEN
Of the generation which will
explore the New Frontier and
others still ahead

Library of Congress Catalog Card Number: 61-7811

SBN—531—00066—X

Printed in the United States of America by **The Garrison Corp.**

THE FIRST BOOK OF THE
WAR OF 1812

RICHARD B. MORRIS

ILLUSTRATED BY LEONARD EVERETT FISHER

FRANKLIN WATTS, INC.
575 Lexington Avenue • New York 22

Copyright © 1961 by Franklin Watts, Inc.

CONTENTS

A Strange War	1
Why the War Was Important	2
Former Foes Become Friends	3
How the Napoleonic Wars Affected America	6
The Tiger and the Shark	7
Impressment	8
"Great Bunglers, Indeed"	9
Jefferson's Embargo	12
Napoleon Tricks Madison	15
Canada, the West, and the "War Hawks"	17
Tippecanoe: Blood Before War	19
War Is Declared	22
The Wrong Fight at the Wrong Place	24
Detroit Falls	26
Disaster at Niagara	27
Lessons from the Disasters of 1812	28
Early Victories at Sea	29
New England Objects to the War	33
The British Lay Down a Blockade	35
Lawrence and the *Chesapeake*	36
American Victories in the North	38
The Battle of Lake Erie	39
The Battle of the Thames	40
New Setbacks in the North	41
The British Mount an Offensive	44
Invasion from the North: The Battle of Lake Champlain	45
The Burning of Washington	48
"The Star-Spangled Banner"	50
War in the South: The Victory at New Orleans	51
The Peacemakers at Ghent	58
Dawn of a New Era	61
Index	62

A STRANGE WAR

America's second war with England was the strangest war she ever fought. If there had been an Atlantic cable, perhaps the United States would never have gone to war at all, for two days before Congress voted for war, the British agreed to one of America's two chief demands. But Congress had not heard about it. Nor, had there been a cable would the United States have won her greatest victory, Andrew Jackson's triumph at New Orleans. This famous battle took place two weeks after America had signed a treaty of peace with England in a little town in Flanders. In those days dispatches were carried by sailing vessels, which took many weeks to cross the Atlantic Ocean.

America's second war with England was strange, too, for a different reason. She had as many causes for going to war against France as she did against England. France, then ruled by Napoleon Bonaparte, a dictator bent on conquering all of Europe, was guilty of as many wrongs against the United States as was England. But the United States chose to go to war with England, and by so doing gave aid and comfort to the French.

Stranger still, the War of 1812 was the only war the American people ever fought against a foreign nation at a time when their own country was sharply divided. The United States went to war to protect the shipping and trade of New England, but New Englanders did not want the war. They did what they could to stop the war. Many of them helped England with dollars and food, and some even thought about breaking away from the Union.

1

WHY THE WAR WAS IMPORTANT

The War of 1812 did not settle a single issue that had caused the United States and England to fight, but when it ended, the two countries were better friends than they had been since the United States became an independent nation. The war might have been a real disaster for America. She entered it without preparing for it. Her attempt to conquer Canada failed. Her own capital was seized and burnt. Her navy was swept off the seas. But she drove the British off American soil and performed heroic deeds on land and sea.

The story of the War of 1812 is a story of men who performed brave deeds out of love for their country. It is the story of the dying Captain Lawrence urging his men aboard the *Chesapeake:* "Don't give up the ship!" — of the youthful Oliver Hazard Perry transferring his flag to the *Niagara* when his own ship, the *Lawrence,* was shot to pieces. Americans will always remember Francis Scott Key writing "The Star Spangled Banner" by the rockets' red glare over gallant Fort McHenry. They are not likely to forget Andrew Jackson and his Kentucky riflemen standing up to the veteran British regulars at New Orleans and cutting the attackers to ribbons.

During the War of 1812 America grew from youth to manhood. In fact, it was not until after the war that the United States became a strong nation, one that the world respected.

FORMER FOES BECOME FRIENDS

The causes of the War of 1812 go back a good many years. America had fought and won a long war against England for her freedom, but even after the peace treaty was signed in 1783 neither side completely carried out all the terms. England held on to the forts on the frontier. The American states took over the property of Tories — Americans who had been loyal to King George III. In some cases Americans refused to pay debts owing to British businessmen.

France was America's old ally, the nation who had helped her win her independence. When France went to war with England in 1793, many Americans felt that they ought to be on her side. But George Washington, the first President of the United States, knew that his country was too weak to get mixed up in a new war. He asked all Americans to remain neutral — not to take sides.

It is very hard indeed not to take sides when a big war breaks out. Many Americans were shocked when the French put their king to death and started a reign of terror against so-called enemies of the French Republic. The revolution in France was much bloodier than America's revolution, and some Americans felt that it was getting out of hand.

On the other hand, a good many other Americans were angered when England, seeking to blockade France, seized American ships and impressed American seamen into her navy. The English navy took such steps because many English sailors were deserting the Royal Navy. They preferred to work for higher wages on American merchant ships. Since both Americans and Englishmen spoke the same language it was often hard to tell who was an Englishman and who was an American. Mistakes were made, and tempers rose.

President Washington believed, however, that trade with England was necessary to America's prosperity. War would end that trade and upset business in the United States. He, therefore, sent the Chief Justice of the United States, a famous patriot named John Jay, to England to seek better relations. Jay made a treaty by which the British agreed to get out of the frontier posts. They also agreed to turn over to commissions made up of persons from both countries certain other questions, such as debts and boundary disputes. Other problems were not settled by Jay. The British refused to agree to stop impressing American seamen. That issue remained to trouble the United States in later years.

Many people in America did not like the treaty negotiated by Jay, but when it went into effect in 1795 it marked the beginning of a ten-year period of friendly relations between America and the mother country.

It was a good thing that America and England were then on friendly terms, because Napoleon Bonaparte, for a time, played with the idea of building another great French empire in America.

Spain controlled the territory west of the Mississippi, as well as East and West Florida and New Orleans. That meant that America could not send goods down the Mississippi to the sea without permission. In 1795, the United States secured from the Spanish the right to deposit goods at New Orleans, and then ship them out.

A famous patriot named John Jay.

Then suddenly and secretly in 1800, Spain turned Louisiana over to France. But before she did so, she took steps to forbid Americans from depositing goods in New Orleans. Thomas Jefferson, newly-elected President of the United States, had always been friendly to France and suspicious of England, but now he declared: "The day that France takes New Orleans we must marry ourselves to the British fleet and nation."

By this remark he meant that America would be willing to make an alliance with England to keep France from controlling the Mississippi and building up a new empire in America. Fortunately, this was not necessary. Napoleon suddenly changed his mind. He gave up the idea of building an empire in the New World and sold Louisiana to the United States for fifteen million dollars. He needed the money to start a new war against England.

HOW THE NAPOLEONIC WARS AFFECTED AMERICA

Since the year 1795, Great Britain had been carrying on a long struggle with France. American shippers profited very much from England's troubles. The Stars and Stripes began to replace the Union Jack on the high seas. Between 1795 and 1806, America's trade with foreign nations jumped threefold. British seamen in growing numbers deserted the Royal Navy to secure higher pay on American merchant ships.

Because French merchant ships had been driven off the seas by England, France encouraged American ships to trade with her West Indian islands. During an earlier war with France, the British courts had laid down the Rule of 1756, which held that no ship, during time of war, could engage in trade forbidden to it in time of peace. France, in peacetime, had forbidden America to trade with her colonies; but now the French allowed Americans to bring sugar from the French West Indies to the United States, pay a duty on the sugar, and then reship it, after the duty had been paid back to the American shipper by France, as American sugar. As neutral cargo, such sugar could be free from seizure by the British.

At first, the British courts held that this practice was not illegal because the voyage had been "broken" by the stop in an American port. But when English shippers protested, the British courts handed down a new opinion that such trade was illegal even though the voyage had been broken in America. When the Royal Navy seized an American ship engaged in such trade with the

French sugar islands, the English courts confiscated the ship and the cargo.

THE TIGER AND THE SHARK

The war between France and England has been compared to a battle between a tiger and a shark. One was supreme on land, the other at sea. The events of the year 1805 proved this. In October of that year Lord Nelson won a great victory over the combined French and Spanish fleets at Trafalgar and ended France's power on the seas. Napoleon now had to give up any idea of crossing the English Channel and invading England.

On land the story was different. Early in December Napoleon crushed the combined armies of Austria and Russia at the great Battle of Austerlitz. The little Corsican now was the supreme ruler on the European continent.

It is very hard for a sea power to fight a land power. About the only course open to a sea power is to impose a blockade on her enemy to keep him from getting supplies from neutral nations. England now took such steps by issuing what are called Orders in Council. These orders told neutrals that they would not be allowed to go directly to a French port; they would have to stop first at a British port.

Napoleon was furious. He declared that any neutral merchant ship that entered a British port would be seized by the French. He vowed to starve England to her knees.

Each side now declared that the other was blockaded. England tightened her blockade of the European continent. Napoleon said

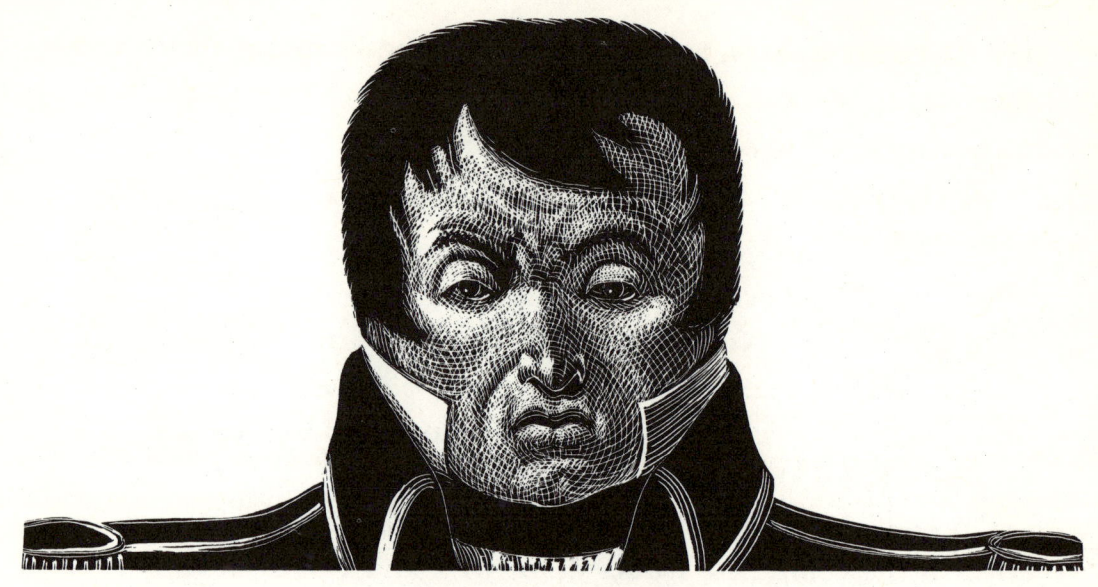

Napoleon was furious.

he would confiscate any ship that obeyed Britain's blockade orders. The side that was best able to put its blockade into operation was the one with the stronger navy. That was England. England was able to hurt the neutrals more than France could, neutrals like the Yankee shippers who ran the risk of violating these blockades.

IMPRESSMENT

The British not only seized ships — they continued to impress seamen aboard American ships. Some of those taken were Englishmen who had obtained papers falsely from American seamen. Both Yankee shippers and the United States Navy encouraged British seamen to desert from the Royal Navy by offering higher pay. Then these seamen were given papers stating that they were Americans. The British naval officers insisted: "Once an Englishman, always an Englishman."

There were two sides to this argument. Many American seamen were impressed. They were given little or no chance to prove that they were not really British deserters. Some six thousand American citizens are believed to have been forced to go into the Royal Navy between 1808 and 1811. In addition, England had been impressing America's seamen for a long time before that.

The American government looked upon impressment as a violation of the rights of neutrals, while the Yankee shipowners and merchants who stayed at home were willing to have American seamen continue to take these risks because the profits from the trading voyages were so huge.

"GREAT BUNGLERS, INDEED"

President Jefferson was anxious to straighten out these difficulties. "No two countries upon earth have so many points in common," he wrote of Great Britain and the United States. "Their rulers must be great bunglers, indeed," he said, if they broke apart. But there was much bungling, and the two countries did break apart. At first Jefferson tried hard to keep them together. He sent two commissioners to England, but the British would not give up any right they claimed. The treaty that the commissioners made was so disappointing that Jefferson never sent it to the Senate.

Many American seame

re impressed.

JEFFERSON'S EMBARGO

Only a few months after Jefferson received the bad news from England, the nation was shocked by an incident that took place outside the three-mile limit off Norfolk Roads. On June 22, 1807, the U.S. frigate *Chesapeake* was hailed by the British frigate *Leopard.* The British captain claimed that four men aboard the American ship were deserters, and demanded the right to search the vessel. The American commander refused. Then the *Leopard* opened fire, killing three of the American crew and wounding eighteen others. The four so-called deserters were removed.

The *Chesapeake* never fired a shot in return, but limped back to port. Years before, Jefferson had said that it "would be a foolish and wicked waste of the energies of our countrymen" to build a big navy.

Jefferson may now have regretted that he had kept the nation weak, but he still tried to have the wrongs on the seas righted without shedding blood. He felt that he had another weapon at hand. At his request, Congress passed the Embargo Act in 1807. This law forbade all land or seaborne commerce with foreign nations. American ships were not permitted to leave for foreign ports, and foreign ships were not allowed to carry goods out of an American port.

As a result of this law, the ports of New England were clogged with idle ships. Many seamen were out of work. In short, a law passed to help New England turned out to hurt her instead.

Fortunately, some New Englanders began to build factories and

The *Leopard* opened fire.

to manufacture the goods they had previously bought from England. The embargo really marked the start of New England as a great factory region. The South was actually hurt more by the embargo than was New England. The planters did not have factories. Therefore, with no way to ship their cotton and tobacco abroad, they found it piling up.

Nevertheless, the chief complaints against the Embargo Act came from the North. Critics of that law shifted the letters around, calling it "O-Grab-Me," or "Go Bar 'Em." Others smuggled goods across the Canadian border. One New Hampshire poet declared:

> Our ships all in motion
> Once whiten'd the ocean:
>   They sail'd and return'd with a Cargo;
> Now doom'd to decay
>   They are fallen a prey,
> To Jefferson, worms, and EMBARGO.

State legislatures stated that the embargo violated the Constitution, and one New Englander, Timothy Pickering, a political enemy of Jefferson, proposed that a meeting of the New England states be held to declare the Embargo Act null and void.

Jefferson and Congress now saw that some changes in the Embargo Act had to be made. It was replaced in 1809 by the Non-Intercourse Act. This new law reopened trade with all nations except France and Great Britain, and gave the President the power to proclaim the renewal of trade with either of those two nations if and when either should stop her violations of American rights on the seas.

This was the situation when James Madison, Jefferson's close friend and Secretary of State, became President. Madison secured a promise from the British Minister to the United States, David M. Erskine, that England would revoke the Orders in Council which forbade neutrals to go to a French port without first stopping at a British port. But the British government would not back up their own minister. They replaced him with an insufferable snob named Francis James Jackson.

Jackson arrived with a coach and four and a retinue of servants. When he saw the new, fast-growing city of Washington, with its muddy roads and severe climate, he thought he was in the backwoods. He found President Madison "a plain and rather mean-looking little man," and he did not get along with him at all. He caused so much trouble that the United States demanded that he be called back to England. The attempts to settle the quarrel by face-to-face talks broke down.

NAPOLEON TRICKS MADISON

Madison had failed to bring about peace with England. He now turned to France. The French government had issued two different kinds of orders or decrees against neutral shipping. The so-called Berlin Decree, issued in 1806, had declared the British Isles in a state of blockade. But this decree was a scrap of paper since Napoleon did not have the fleet to enforce it. Other decrees issued by Napoleon did hurt American shipping. These decrees ordered that any neutral ship that obeyed the British Orders in Council or first went to a British port should be seized at sea or in port.

Congress now gave France and England a chance to mend their ways before it was too late. In 1810, Nathaniel Macon, a Congressman from North Carolina, had Congress replace the Non-Intercourse Act with a new bill, known ever since as *Macon's Bill No. 2.* It gave President Madison the power to reopen trade with England and France. Should either country, before March 3, 1811, change or revoke its edicts and stop its violations of American shipping, the President was given the power to forbid Americans to trade with the other country.

When Napoleon learned of Macon's Bill No. 2, he had his Foreign Minister, the Duc de Cadore, notify the American Minister in Paris that France had abolished her trade decrees. Madison took Napoleon at his word and proclaimed the opening of trade with France, but announced that trade with England would come to a halt on February 2, 1811, because that nation had not withdrawn her decrees. The facts are that Napoleon did not publish his new edict until he was forced to, and that was over a year later. He had tricked Madison into pushing America into war with England, Bonaparte's great enemy.

The British government knew that Madison had been tricked, and decided to act tougher than ever before toward the United States. The 38-gun British frigate *Guerrière* overhauled an American brig off Sandy Hook and impressed a native-born American. Captain John Rodgers, commanding the U.S. 44-gun frigate *President,* was ordered to cruise off Sandy Hook to protect American ships. He sighted a ship that he thought was the *Guerrière,* but it actually was a 20-gun British corvette, *Little Belt.* The

President gave chase and her guns pounded the smaller ship and put it out of action.

The British press sizzled. "Insolence must be punished!" their newspapers screamed. Napoleon's trick had worked very well indeed. America and England were on the verge of war. The little Corsican had outsmarted President Madison.

CANADA, THE WEST, AND THE "WAR HAWKS"

Ever since the Revolution, American settlers had been pushing into the West. In 1794, General Anthony Wayne defeated the Indians at the Battle of Fallen Timbers, and in the same year the British gave up their control of the western forts. It looked as though the threat of the Indians would no longer hang over the heads of the pioneers.

But there was a new spirit among the Indians. New leaders, seeing large tracts of land being taken up by the white man, felt that unless the Indians took a stand, they would be pushed out of the prairie country. Greatest of the new Indian leaders was the Shawnee chief Tecumseh, the "Shooting Star" or "Crouching Panther," who set out to organize all the Indian tribes.

The white men, too, were finding new leaders. These were a group of young members of Congress from the South and West, called the "war hawks" because they seemed so bold and fierce. Most of them were in their thirties; none was over forty. Chief among them was a Virginia-born Kentuckian named Henry Clay, who was elected the new Speaker of the House of Representatives. Tennessee sent a "war hawk" named Felix Grundy to Congress.

Chief among them was a Virginia-born Kentuckian named Henry Clay.

Western New York was represented by Peter B. Porter, and South Carolina had three young fire-eaters, William Lowndes, Langdon Cheves, and John C. Calhoun. Calhoun was destined to be the most famous statesman ever to come from that state.

Why was it that most of the "war hawks" came from the farm country of the South and West instead of from the coastal areas, which were hardest hit by the British Orders in Council? It was because people in the South and West were terribly worried about the Indians on the frontier. They felt that unless Canada was wrested from England, and Florida from Spain — England's ally — there would be no chance for settlers to build homes along the frontier. These "war hawks" spoke not only for themselves, but also for the northern farmers who wanted Canada and the southern farmers who wanted Florida.

The western farmers were also hurt by the decrees of England and France, as well as by the American embargo. They could no longer sell their farm products overseas. Times were hard on the farms, and the farmers blamed the British.

TIPPECANOE: BLOOD BEFORE WAR

The War of 1812 started in the backwoods of the Old Northwest. The Indians were not allowed to forget their resentment of the advance of the Americans because Tecumseh kept reminding them that they must unite and fight back. His brother, Lalawethika, was known as the "Prophet" because he claimed to have had a vision in which the Great Spirit told him to lead a crusade against the white man and his ways. Together the brothers organized a great confederacy of Indian tribes to block the westward push of America.

In 1811, the governor of the Indiana Territory, William Henry Harrison, gathered a military force to break up the Indian Confederacy. He wanted first of all to destroy the Prophet's town, the Indian capital on Tippecanoe Creek. He led his men from Vincennes and encamped about a mile from the Indian village. Then the Indians made a surprise attack at dawn, but the Americans, fighting fiercely though suffering heavily, drove the Indians back and set fire to the village and the food supply. The West hailed this as a great victory, but it was hardly that. The battle made Governor Harrison famous, and many years later he was elected President of the United States on his record as a military hero.

Harrison had failed to end the warlike activities either of the

The Indians made

prise attack at dawn.

Prophet or of Tecumseh. The West was now convinced that it was in terrible danger and that the English in Canada were egging the Indians on to kill the white settlers. The fact is that the British government had nothing to do with Tecumseh's moves and wanted peace on the frontier as much as did the United States, but American settlers were sure that England and the fur traders were behind all the Indian troubles.

Andrew Jackson, then commanding a Tennessee militia unit, now offered his services against the Tippecanoe Indians. He declared: "That banditti ought to be swept off the face of the earth." A great many people in the West who felt like Jackson welcomed a war with England.

WAR IS DECLARED

The British were stubborn and foolishly gave America a reason for going to war when they refused to revoke their Orders in Council. President Madison felt that America no longer had a choice, and called upon Congress for a declaration of war against England. The vote was close. In the Senate it was 19 to 13; in the House 79 to 49. The West and the South voted for war. New York and New England voted against it.

Two days before Congress acted, Great Britain had announced that she had suspended her Orders in Council. The grain crop had failed, and the British were really desperate. They were anxious to get American grain.

It took a good many weeks for sailing ships to carry dispatches across the Atlantic. Congress did not know that it had declared war when there was no longer any reason for doing so. The English had acted too late.

The "war hawks" felt that this would be an easy war. Henry Clay boasted that the militiamen of Kentucky alone could conquer Canada. Former President Jefferson said it was a "mere matter of marching."

On paper, America looked pretty strong. There were almost eight million people in the United States compared with a half million Canadians. And the Canadians were not even united. The French and English settlers spoke different languages. Could England count on the loyalty of the French Canadians? Could England, fighting for her life against Napoleon, spare troops for America? Would the Indians fight on Canada's side? Soon these big questions would be answered.

There were plenty of shocks in store for the "war hawks." Actually the United States was very weak. She never was able to get more than seven thousand regulars and militia into any one battle. Her army was small and scattered, the state militia poorly trained and unreliable. Her navy was tiny. She had only twenty vessels and some gunboats, while England had six hundred fighting ships even though she could only spare a small portion of her fleet for duty in the Western Atlantic. Many people opposed the war, particularly in New England. The United States started with old and feeble generals, and it took her a long time to find good ones. Meantime, President Madison and his Cabinet showed poor leadership. Since the United States did not have a central bank, she had to borrow money by public subscription, but almost half of the bonds remained unsold. To top it all, the United States' plan of military operations was a very poor one.

THE WRONG FIGHT AT THE WRONG PLACE

In the first period of the war the United States took the offensive. England was locked on the European continent in a terrible struggle with Napoleon, and could not spare a big force to fight in North America.

The American war strategy was simple but wrong — a quick knockout blow against Canada. Several invasion routes into Canada were available. Had the Americans invaded by way of Lake Champlain and the Richelieu River and seized Montreal, they would have cut Canada's line of communications from the sea and the St. Lawrence to Upper Canada. That province could not have held out. But this invasion route meant going through an area inhabited by Americans not friendly to the war.

Another possible invasion route was not seriously considered. That was a march through the Maine wilderness to capture the great fortress of Quebec, key to the whole St. Lawrence Valley. The Americans had suffered a tragic defeat at Quebec early in the American Revolution, and they felt that the defenses of this city were too strong.

Instead, the Americans concentrated on the West. There the war spirit among Americans ran higher, and the Canadian forces were weak. This looked like the softest spot to hit.

Most of the fighting in the first period of the war took place between the western end of Lake Ontario and the western end

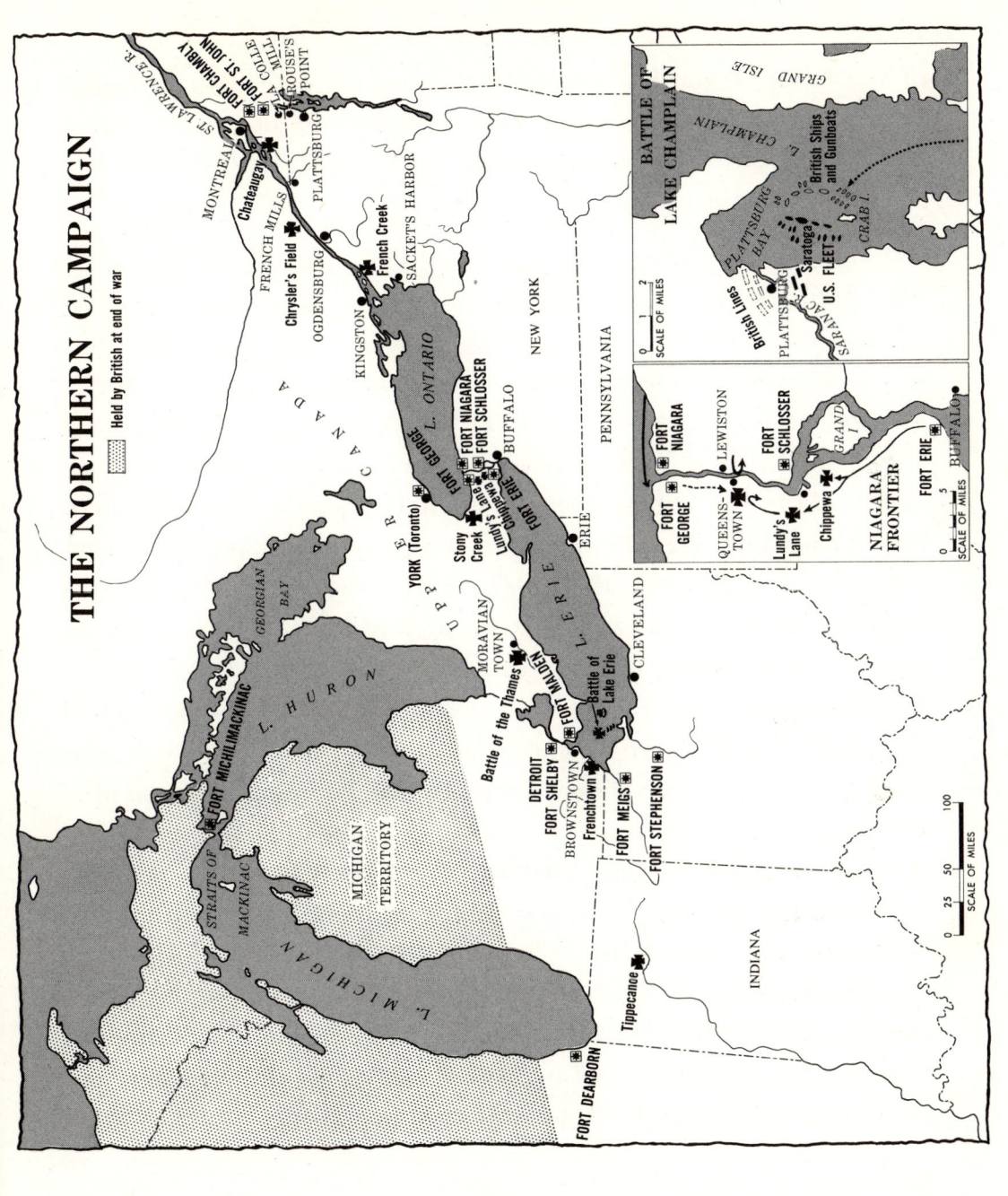

of Lake Erie, roughly between Fort Niagara and Detroit. Using poor strategy, the Americans sought victories where they would make little difference to the outcome of the war. In addition, they scattered their forces instead of uniting them for one big blow against the North.

DETROIT FALLS

The American campaign got off to a very bad start. The first drive in the West was under the command of an aged and infirm general named William Hull. He had been a dashing young officer in the Revolution, but now he was timid and cautious. Across the river from American-held Detroit lay the Canadian Fort Malden. Had Hull struck quickly, it would have fallen. Instead, he waited while British General Isaac Brock assembled a mixed force of Canadians, British, and Indians. Brock, a brave, driving man, moved his men quickly across the river from Fort Malden and cut Hull's line of communication with Ohio. Then he brought up his artillery and laid siege to Detroit. Brock sent Hull a message under a flag of truce to say he "might not be able to control the Indians" if he was forced to take the place by storm.

Hull seemed paralyzed by fear. There were women and children in Detroit, and he did not want harm to come to them. When a shot from a British ship fell into the fort and killed two men on August 16, 1812, Hull, in a weak voice, gave the order to hoist a white flag. He was tried by court-martial and sentenced to death for cowardice and neglect of duty, but the sentence was never carried out. Instead, he was dropped from the army rolls.

Hull, in a weak voice, gave the order to hoist a white flag.

Even before Hull surrendered Detroit, the American fort on Michilimackinac Island, at the juncture of Lakes Michigan and Huron, had fallen to the British on July 17. Then, on August 15, the day before Brock took Detroit, the small American garrison at Fort Dearborn, the present Chicago, was abandoned on orders of Hull. When the garrison tried to make its way across the Michigan Peninsula to Detroit, it was set upon by Indians and massacred. A few bold, swift strokes, and the whole American territory north and west of Ohio had fallen to the enemy.

DISASTER AT NIAGARA

Immediately after taking Detroit, Brock transferred most of his forces to the Niagara frontier. There the American command was divided between General Stephen Van Rensselaer, who assembled a force of New York militiamen, and General Alexander

Smyth, who commanded the Regular Army troops. Van Rensselaer owed his command to the fact that he was a great landowner in New York. His rival, Smyth, was a boastful politician with little nerve and no ability.

Van Rensselaer attacked the Canadian village of Queenston across the Niagara River on October 13. His men clambered to the heights above the village. Then Brock's men counterattacked, and Brock himself was killed. Van Rensselaer managed to put some nine hundred men, mostly Regulars, across the river. He was in sight of victory, when the rest of his force, the militiamen, refused to cross over. They claimed that they were only obliged to defend the state, not to invade foreign territory. This left the Regulars without support, and they were killed or captured when British and Canadian reinforcements reached Queenston.

Smyth, who now replaced Van Rensselaer as commander of the New York militia, started across the Niagara River, then got cold feet and pulled back. He was dropped from the army rolls. At the same time General Henry Dearborn, commanding the largest force of Americans under arms, led his men from Plattsburg on Lake Champlain to the Canadian frontier for an attack on Montreal. Again the militia refused to cross over into Canada. So Dearborn led his army back to Plattsburg. Two more attacks. Result: zero.

LESSONS FROM THE DISASTERS OF 1812

The first year of the war on land had taught the American people a bitter lesson. One cannot go to war without being properly prepared, without a properly trained army, and without being properly led. President Madison had to learn the hard way how to run a war. He now saw that the nation needed a sizable army of regular troops who would obey orders under able commanders.

The first thing Madison did was to oust the Secretary of War, William Eustis, and replace him with a veteran of the Revolution named John Armstrong. Armstrong, who had little use for the President, was known as a troublemaker, and he proved to be a failure as a War Secretary. The year 1812 had shown that the American army could not as yet successfully invade enemy soil. How would it stand up against an invasion of its own country?

EARLY VICTORIES AT SEA

Although the land campaigns of 1812 brought little credit to the army, the war at sea brought glory to the young American navy, and gave the public a constellation of heroes. The little fleet of heavily armed and stoutly built American frigates engaged the British navy in a series of individual duels, ship against ship. The British, who had not tasted defeat on the high seas for many a year, were astounded by the American victories.

The first shock to the British occurred on August 19, 1812, when Captain Isaac Hull's 44-gun *Constitution* outfought and sank the British frigate *Guerrière* off Nova Scotia. Hull counted on firepower and marksmanship. Seemingly without a nerve in his body, he held his fire until he could work into close quarters with the enemy ship. Shots were ripping through the rigging of

Captain Isaac Hull's 44-gun *Constitution* outfoug

d sank the British frigate *Guerriere*.

the *Constitution* and cutting splinters from her masts and spars. But every one of her guns remained silent. When the *Constitution* drew within fifty yards of the enemy, Hull shouted: "Now, boys, pour it into them!"

Every gun in the frigate's battery went off. The *Guerrière* trembled. Her mizzenmast fell over the side. Her cockpit was full of wounded. Then Hull ordered the gunners to aim for the yellow streak where the British gun-ports were. The *Guerrière*'s two other masts pitched into the sea, and she lay helpless. The British flag fluttered to the frigate's deck, and Hull took possession. It must be remembered that in those days it was considered no disgrace to surrender a ship when the situation was hopeless, as was the case here.

The remarkable string of American victories at sea could be credited to the ability of the Americans to fight well at close range, to their accurate marksmanship, and to the fact that American crews were better trained than British crews and American ships were better handled in battle.

Captain Jacob Jones's *Wasp* bested the British 18-gun *Frolic,* but then he lost his own ship to the *Poictiers.* The big 44-gun frigate *United States,* commanded by the fiery Captain Stephen Decatur, captured the frigate *Macedonian* off the Madeira Islands and brought her into New London as a prize. Under her new commander, Captain William Bainbridge, the *Constitution* destroyed the British frigate *Java* in a duel off the coast of Brazil.

Her successes during the war earned for the *Constitution* the affectionate nickname of "Old Ironsides." The nickname referred to the ship's ability to take punishment. Real ironclad vessels were not used in naval warfare until the Civil War. Some years after the War of 1812 had ended, the navy planned to break up the old ship. Dr. Oliver Wendell Holmes, then a young man of twenty-one, wrote a famous poem that every schoolboy used to know. It began:

> Ay, tear her tattered ensign down!
> Long has it waved on high.

As a result of his poem the old wooden ship was preserved.

Still another American victory followed the first four. The American *Hornet,* under the command of the bold and popular James Lawrence, sank the British *Peacock.* Five one-sided victories in a row. The British were stunned. Their government ordered her frigates to avoid individual fights with the bigger American fighting ships, and to engage them two against one. From then on, the British navy was to make its power felt by overwhelming numbers of ships, guns, and seamen.

NEW ENGLAND OBJECTS TO THE WAR

News that war was declared was received grimly in New England, which had long suffered from the embargo and the stoppage of her commerce. The governor of Massachusetts declared a public fast in view of the breaking out of war "against the nation from which we are descended." This hardly sounded like the minutemen at Lexington and Concord who fought off the Redcoats. But opposition to the war spread in Yankeeland, from state to state. New England and New York contractors supplied beef, flour, and other provisions to the British armies in Canada and to enemy vessels off the East Coast. Finally, President Madison asked Congress to forbid trade with the enemy. But even when such trade was forbidden by law, dealings across the Canadian border continued.

Despite his poor showing in the early part of the war and the opposition to him in the North, James Madison was elected President again in 1812. But it was by a very close vote in a campaign against De Witt Clinton of New York. Clinton carried all of New England and the Middle States, with the exception of Vermont and Pennsylvania. Throughout most of his second term Madison presided over a divided country. The North was against the war; the South and West were for it.

In October, 1814, delegates from the New England states met at Hartford, Connecticut. Some who attended would have seceded from the Union, but fortunately saner counsels prevailed. The Convention adopted resolutions demanding a two-thirds vote of both Houses of Congress for declaring war, limiting the President to one term, and suggesting various reforms which would have crippled the ability of the federal government to declare and wage war.

News of the ending of the war cut short the activities of the Hartford group. Those who gathered at Hartford were laughed at by some and considered traitors by others. Fortunately for the nation, New England stayed in the Union.

THE BRITISH LAY DOWN A BLOCKADE

Ship for ship the Americans had trounced the British in the first year of the war. Then the British decided to strike back in force. At the end of 1812, the British sent a naval force under Rear Admiral Sir George Cockburn to blockade the Atlantic coast from New York to Savannah. But they did not blockade New England because they hoped to encourage New England to split away from the rest of the country. When this hope did not come true, the British, in 1814, blockaded New England as well. They used the Chesapeake Bay as a naval station. They made it difficult to import goods into the United States. The United States Treasury had counted on the cash receipts from customs duties to run the war. Now, because imports were falling off, the Treasury's cash position was low and the government was in bad financial shape.

The blockade encouraged Americans to manufacture their own goods, and once the war was over, New England was to become a big industrial region. The Americans also dispatched cruisers which captured British merchant convoys and whalers in the Atlantic and South Pacific, and many American privateersmen roamed the seas. These were privately owned armed merchant ships authorized by the government to fight and seize British vessels. By 1814, it was unsafe for British shipping to sail without convoy from the English to the Irish Channel. But these counterpunches did not force the British to loosen their tight blockade of the American coast. By the time the war ended, only a handful of American frigates were still operating. Most of the American privateers had been bottled up in port or driven off the seas.

LAWRENCE AND THE *CHESAPEAKE*

The gloom that hung over the American cause in 1813 was darkened by the news of a naval battle between the 38-gun frigate *Chesapeake* of the U.S. Navy and the British frigate *Shannon*, of equal firepower. The fight took place thirty miles outside of Boston Harbor. Captain P. B. V. Broke of the *Shannon* sent a challenge to James Lawrence, commander of the *Chesapeake,* and Lawrence sailed out of the harbor to meet it. Lawrence had a larger crew, but they were mostly poorly trained foreign seamen who became panic-stricken under fire.

Both ships opened fire at the same time. Both were hit hard, but the *Chesapeake* suffered the most. The frigates were close enough for musket shots. Lawrence was shot through the lungs, the first lieutenant was killed by a cannon ball, the man at the wheel was shot. A hand grenade exploded in the *Chesapeake*'s arms-chest, and the chest blew up.

Broke led a British boarding party onto the American frigate. Below, in the cockpit, the dying Lawrence heard the tramp of feet above his head. "Don't give up the ship!" he cried. A second lieutenant led a gallant countercharge. Broke was wounded, but it was too late to save the *Chesapeake.* The British took her into Halifax as a prize. Lawrence's dying words became the rallying cry of the American navy.

"Don't give up the ship!" he cried.

AMERICAN VICTORIES IN THE NORTH

During the second year of the war, the Americans tried to recapture Detroit and to mount an attack on Canada across Lake Ontario. For the Detroit campaign the American troops were placed under the command of Brigadier General William Henry Harrison, the hero of Tippecanoe. Harrison started north toward Lake Erie at the end of October, 1812, with some 4,500 men. A detachment of a thousand men pushed forward to a point nearly opposite Fort Malden. There they were defeated and massacred by a slightly larger force of Canadians and Indians. Then winter forced Harrison to postpone further operations.

The Ontario campaign was under the command of General Henry Dearborn. On April 22, 1813, he embarked 1,700 men and sailed up Lake Ontario. He arrived off York (now Toronto), the capital of Upper Canada, where on April 27, his men seized the fort midway between the town and the landing. Just as the Americans were pushing through the fort a powder magazine or mine exploded. Many American and British soldiers were killed, including American Brigadier General Zebulon Pike, the famous explorer of the Southwest and discoverer of Pikes Peak. The American troops then got out of hand. They looted or burned public buildings in York and destroyed the records of the province. After holding the town for about a week, Dearborn's forces crossed over the lake to Niagara to join an attack by Colonel Winfield Scott against the forts on the Canadian side of the Niagara River.

While the Americans were raiding York, Sir George Prevost, the Governor General of Canada, on May 28, launched an attack from Kingston on Sackett's Harbor on the New York side of Lake Ontario. The American defenders were commanded by a Quaker farmer, Brigadier General Jacob Brown of the New York militia. The British routed the first line, but the second line held and threw back the British with heavy losses. Then Brown sent the New York militia toward the rear of the enemy's right flank. The British were afraid they would be cut off, so they pulled back to their ships after taking a severe drubbing. Brown had shown the ablest generalship of any American commander on the northern front thus far.

On the same day that Prevost's forces sailed against Sackett's Harbor, Dearborn's forces landed from Lake Ontario and seized Fort George on the Niagara River. But Dearborn failed to follow up his victory. Part of his command ventured outside the fort and were trapped by the British and Indians. For the rest of the year the war on the Niagara front remained a stalemate. Dearborn, who was ailing in health and lacked drive and daring, resigned his commission.

THE BATTLE OF LAKE ERIE

Hull had lost Detroit in 1812, and Harrison had made little headway in getting it back the following year. These failures made it clear that the Americans must gain control of Lake Erie before they could hope to recapture the city. Twenty-eight-year-old Captain Oliver Hazard Perry was ordered to oversee the building of a fleet and to seize control of the lake.

Throughout the spring and summer of 1813, the young captain was busy at Erie, Pennsylvania, assembling his fleet, guns, and crews. By the beginning of August he was ready. He sailed up the lake and anchored in Put-in-Bay, near the line still held by General Harrison. There, on September 10, Perry met the British fleet. The longer range of the British guns soon battered Perry's flagship, the *Lawrence.* All of Perry's officers were killed or wounded, but he refused to give up. He took a small boat, and at the height of the battle was rowed over to the *Niagara,* which he now took over as his flagship. Perry brought the *Niagara*'s powerful guns to bear on the two big British ships. Soon the British ships were in distress, and the entire British fleet surrendered. In fifteen minutes Perry had turned his seeming defeat into victory and gained control of Lake Erie. Then he sat down and on the back of an old envelope wrote this message to General Harrison:

Dear General:
    We have met the enemy and they are ours: two ships, two brigs, one schooner, and one sloop.
    Yours with great respect and esteem,

                                          O. H. Perry

THE BATTLE OF THE THAMES

With Lake Erie cleared of the British, Harrison now embarked his army and sailed against Fort Malden. A regiment of Kentucky mounted riflemen, commanded by Colonel Richard M. Johnson, moved along the shore of the lake toward Detroit. In the face of this double threat the British abandoned both Forts Malden and Detroit and retreated eastward. Harrison caught up with them on the banks of the Thames River about eighty-five miles from Malden. There he surprised a mixed force of 900 British Regulars and 2,000 Indians. Instead of attacking with infantry, he ordered Colonel Johnson to rip into the enemy with his cavalry. Most of the British surrendered. The Indians fled to the woods, where the Kentuckians dismounted and fought with them hand-to-hand. The Indians were completely routed. Tecumseh was killed, fighting to the last, but his body has never been found. This battle shattered the Indian confederacy and ended the war on this front.

NEW SETBACKS IN THE NORTH

One of the United States' biggest failures of the war was the expedition launched against Montreal in the fall of 1813. One group of six thousand men were to attack down the St. Lawrence River from Sackett's Harbor. They were placed under the command of Major General James Wilkinson, a friend of Secretary of War Armstrong. Wilkinson had a very bad reputation. A number of years before, he had conspired with Aaron Burr to seize New Orleans and carve an empire out of the Southwest. He then turned against Burr and denounced him. Wilkinson was tried and acquitted, but everyone continued to suspect him. The facts later came out that he had received a pension from the Spanish government. His name appeared on the Spanish account

"We have met the ene

they are ours."

books as "Spy No. 13." This was the man chosen to head a big United States expedition!

A second force was supposed to move north against Montreal from Lake Champlain. This force was placed under the command of General Wade Hampton of South Carolina. Hampton hated and despised Wilkinson, and it was clear that they could not work together. Separately they did not have the strength to capture Montreal. Wilkinson's men were thrown back about ninety miles from that Canadian city, and Hampton never got started. At the very end of the year the British, in revenge for the burning and looting of Canadian towns by the Americans, seized Fort Niagara and burned Buffalo. As the year 1813 ended, the war in the North was still very much a seesaw affair.

THE BRITISH MOUNT AN OFFENSIVE

Early in 1814, Napoleon Bonaparte was overthrown. England was now free to throw all of her vast strength into the war in North America. During the summer of 1814, fourteen thousand British troops who had fought Napoleon under the Duke of Wellington were sent across the Atlantic. On paper the British had an excellent plan to crush the United States and end the war. They planned to thrust south into New York State through Lake Champlain. Another invasion army was to move against Washington and Baltimore from the Chesapeake Bay, and a third attack was to seize New Orleans and get control of the Mississippi River. To support this triple attack of naval and land forces the British now tightened the blockade of the American coast.

The United States was better prepared to meet such an attack than it would have been in 1812. The regular army had been greatly increased. Wilkinson and other incompetent generals had been removed from command, and better men had been chosen to lead the fighting forces.

INVASION FROM THE NORTH: THE BATTLE OF LAKE CHAMPLAIN

Before the British could get their invasion under way, the Americans under General Jacob Brown, who took the place of Wilkinson, crossed the Niagara River into Canada and seized Fort Erie. General Riall of the British army drew up his main force on the Chippewa Plain about a mile from the river. Brown sent General Winfield Scott's brigade into action against a slightly larger force. The British lines crumbled.

The Battle of Chippewa was a kind of turning point in the war. After Chippewa, no force of United States regulars was defeated by the British army. Still, the invasion of Canada got nowhere. The Americans under Brown fought the British to a draw in a stubborn battle at Lundy's Lane near Niagara Falls, but then fell back to Fort Erie. The British laid siege to that fort, but the Americans held out and forced the British to withdraw. Then the Americans destroyed the fort and gave up the drive on Canada.

In September, 1814, the big British land and water attack along the Lake Champlain route got under way. The British under Sir George Prevost outnumbered the Americans at Plattsburg, New York, by almost four to one. Unless the United States could control Lake Champlain it was clear that nothing could stop the invaders.

The American naval commander on the lake was the thirty-year-old Captain Thomas Macdonough. He had at his command a flotilla of four ships and ten gunboats. His plan of battle was to arrange his ships in such a way that his powerful short-range guns could do their damage before the long-range guns of the British could blow the American ships out of the lake. Macdonough anchored his fleet in the narrow channel between Crab Island and Cumberland Head, across the bay from Plattsburg. The enemy ships would have to enter a narrow stretch of water under fire and meet him at close range.

The Battle of Lake Champlain (September 11, 1814) lasted two hours and twenty minutes. All of the British vessels except the gunboats were seized or destroyed. During the battle on the lake, Sir George Prevost stood on a hill looking through a glass at the defenses of Plattsburg. An aide-de-camp, who had been down at the shore when the British lowered, or "struck," their flags, rushed up and exclaimed: "They have struck, sir!"

Sir George lowered his glass. "The Americans?"

"No, sir, the whole British fleet."

For Prevost the news meant the end of his dream of conquest. Macdonough's great victory gave the Americans control of Lake Champlain and forced the British to pull their army back to Canada.

"They have struck, sir!"

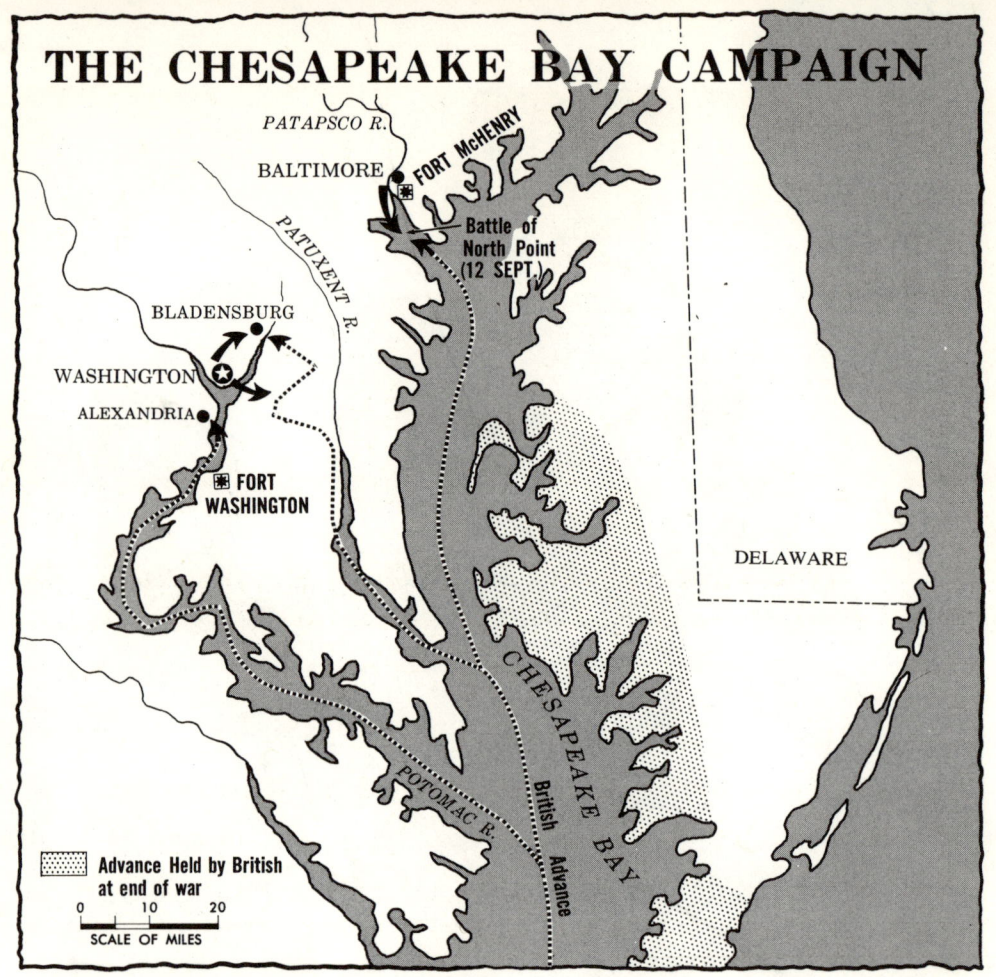

THE BURNING OF WASHINGTON

To keep the United States from sending all her troops to the Canadian border, the British decided to strike at other points. Sir Alexander Cochrane, in command of the British fleet blockading Southern waters, ordered his squadron "to destroy and lay waste" towns along the coast. In August, 1814, the British fleet, along with transports carrying four thousand veteran British troops under General Robert Ross moved up Chesapeake Bay to the

The British . . . set fire to the White House.

mouth of the Patuxent River in Maryland. They landed without encountering any resistance and marched on Washington.

Panic seized the American capital. Heading a mixed force of seven thousand men, of whom only a few hundred were regulars, General William H. Winder tried to stop the British at Bladensburg. The Americans were routed when the militia became panic-stricken. Then Commodore Joshua Barney and his four hundred sailors and marines covered the road. They held the ground for half an hour, outnumbered ten to one. As the British entered Washington, President Madison and other government officials fled from the city. Secretary of War Armstrong went into hiding. The British, in revenge for the burning of York, set fire to the Capitol, the White House, and other government buildings. Then they boarded their transports on the Patuxent River.

The country was bitter and ashamed. The newspapers chanted:

> Fly, Winder, fly! Run, Armstrong, run!
> Were the last words of Madison.

The President forced Armstrong to resign and put in his place James Monroe, who also doubled as Secretary of State. Monroe had more energy and ability than the previous War Secretaries. The results of the change soon made themselves felt.

"THE STAR-SPANGLED BANNER"

Now the British moved on Baltimore, a great port of American privateers. But that city was prepared to meet them. Under General Samuel Smith some thirteen thousand regulars and militia defended the town. A mixed force of a thousand men held Fort McHenry, where a line of sunken hulks barred enemy vessels from the harbor.

The British army under the command of General Ross disembarked about fourteen miles from Baltimore, while the British fleet moved up the river toward Fort McHenry. The enemy push on land was opposed by 3,200 militiamen under General John Stricker. The Americans fell back, but not before severely punishing the enemy. General Ross was mortally wounded.

When the British drew up within sight of the heavily defended heights, they halted and then pulled back to their ships. Having failed to take Baltimore by land, the British fleet now launched a hot bombardment against Fort McHenry, which blocked the approach to Baltimore by water. On the deck of a sailing ship at anchor in the river was a young American lawyer named Francis Scott Key. He paced the deck all night watching the bombardment. At seven o'clock the next morning the British ceased firing. The Stars and Stripes were still flying over Fort McHenry.

Thrilled by the brave defense of the fort, Key jotted down some notes for a song, which he completed when he returned to Baltimore. He wrote the song to the tune of "To Anacreon in Heaven," which had been sung by a musical society in London around the time of the Revolution. Key took the song to his brother-in-law, Judge Joseph Hopper Nicholson, who had been a captain of a gunnery company during the siege. Nicholson liked it so much he sent the poem off to a printer. It was printed first under the title "The Defense of Fort McHenry." And so was born "The Star-Spangled Banner," that inspiring and patriotic song that Americans love dearly.

The British had failed on land and water. Their army left Chesapeake Bay in October and sailed for Jamaica.

WAR IN THE SOUTH: THE VICTORY AT NEW ORLEANS

On the eve of the War of 1812, Tecumseh had visited the Creek Indians in the Alabama Country. He wanted them to join his confederacy. Once the war started, a war party among the Creeks, known as the "Red Sticks" because they were armed with red sticks or war clubs, set the southern frontier ablaze. In August, 1813, the Creeks attacked Fort Mims, situated about thirty-five miles above Mobile, Alabama. Of the 550 persons in the fort,

He paced the deck all ni

atching the bombardment.

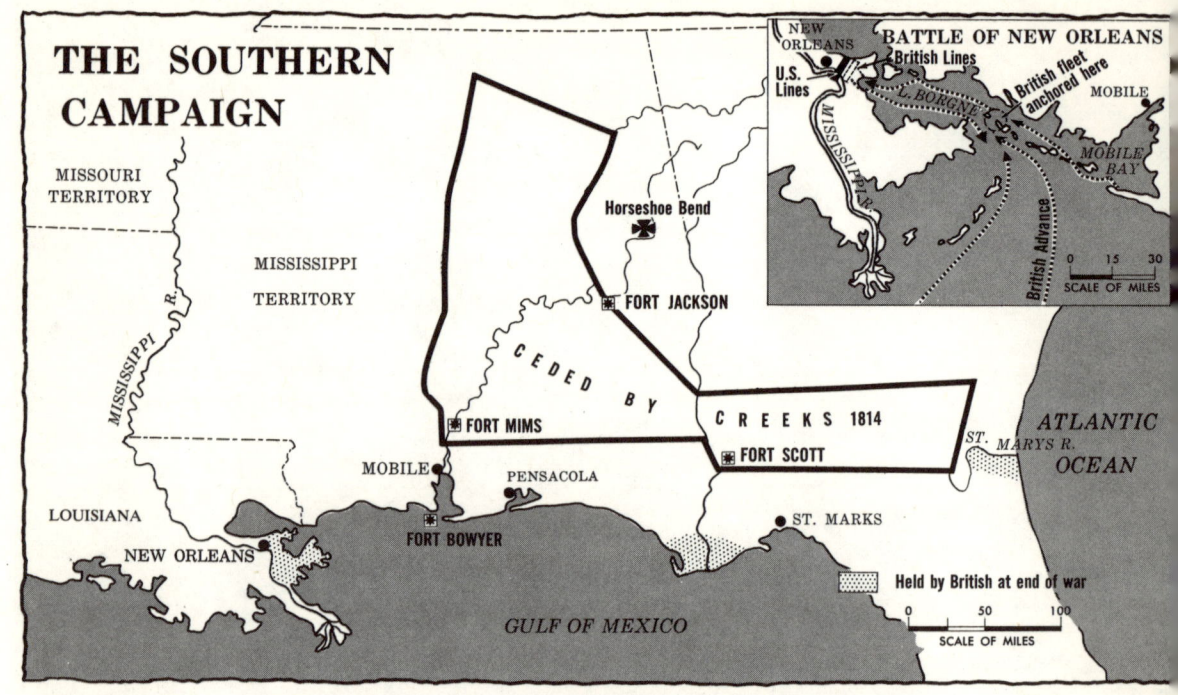

they massacred 250 and burned to death many others.

News of this tragedy reached Andrew Jackson at Nashville, Tennessee. As major general of the Tennessee militia he now had his chance. Jackson called out two thousand volunteers. He carried the fighting into the heart of the Creek country and smashed the Creeks and their Cherokee allies at the Horseshoe Bend of the Tallapoosa River. He made the Creeks agree to turn over a large part of their lands to the United States and to get out of the southern and western part of Alabama.

At the same time another Indian fighter, William Henry Harrison, made peace with the Northwest Indians, who now turned around and declared war on the British. It was indeed a serious blow to the British to lose their brave fighting allies on the northern and southern frontiers. On the other hand, the stubborn Indian fighting had forced the United States to send soldiers, who were badly needed elsewhere, to the South.

It was clear even to the men in Washington that America had found a great soldier in Andrew Jackson. He was bold, swift, and fiery. He expected his orders to be obeyed. Jackson was now given command of the United States army in the Southwest.

At the end of November, a large British fleet carrying 7,500 veterans under Sir Edward Pakenham sailed from Jamaica to attack New Orleans and seize control of the Mississippi River. The British fleet entered Lake Borgne, about forty miles east of New Orleans. An advance guard marched to within seven miles of New Orleans.

Jackson moved fast. On December 23, he led five thousand troops in a night attack on the enemy. After both sides suffered heavy casualties, Jackson withdrew his men to a point five miles from New Orleans. He built a line of breastworks stretching from a cypress swamp to the east bank of the Mississippi. There he waited for the enemy.

On January 8, 1815, Pakenham attacked with his main force of 5,300 men. In Jackson's trenches were about 4,500 troops, many of them crack marksmen from Kentucky and Tennessee armed with the Kentucky long rifle. As a popular song of that day, "The Hunters of Kentucky," celebrated the battle:

> Behind it stood our little force —
> None wished it to be greater;
> For ev'ry man was half a horse,
> And half an alligator.

The British, cheering, advanced bravely to the slaughter. In close ranks they made two direct assaults. Accurate rifle and artillery fire cut them down like blades of grass beneath a scythe. It was all over in half an hour. General Pakenham and two other British generals were killed, and two thousand British soldiers were killed or wounded. The United States losses were eight killed, thirteen wounded. The battered British army pulled out and sailed for home.

At New Orleans the Americans showed that they handled guns better than the British. They had shown this, too, in battles on the Canadian frontier, at Lake Erie and on Lake Champlain. If the American infantry had been as well drilled as the artillery, the war might have been over a lot sooner.

The Battle of New Orleans was America's greatest land victory of the war, but it had no effect on the outcome of the conflict. Two weeks before it was fought peace had been signed, but it took so many weeks for news to travel overseas that neither Pakenham nor Jackson had known that the war was officially over at the time of the Battle of New Orleans. The battle created a great national hero, however, a hero who would some day be president, and it made Americans proud at last of their fighting men. It was a glorious ending to a very strange war.

There he waited for the enemy.

THE PEACEMAKERS AT GHENT

It must be remembered that while England was carrying on the war in America she was also fighting against Napoleon on the Continent. England's ally was Russia. Czar Nicholas I of that country was anxious to end the war between England and the United States so that England could put all her strength into winning the war against Napoleon. When the War of 1812 started, the Czar offered to act as a mediator between the United States and Great Britain — that is, to try to make peace between the two warring nations. But Lord Castlereagh, England's foreign minister, would not accept his offer.

As time went on and England failed to knock America out of the war, Castlereagh began to think more seriously about peace with the United States. When he learned of the British defeat on Lake Erie, he suggested talks to end the war. Madison named as our peace commissioners some of our wisest statesmen, including John Quincy Adams, the son of President John Adams, Henry Clay, the brilliant young Speaker of the House of Representatives, and Albert Gallatin, Swiss-born Secretary of the Treasury. The British commissioners were less important men, but then they were closer to home and could be more easily instructed by their government.

Peace talks began in August, 1814, at the picturesque town of Ghent in Flanders. The American commissioners had been told to insist that the British stop impressment and cease the blockade and other actions on the high seas that Americans considered illegal. In turn, the British commissioners had been told to demand that a neutral Indian state be set up in the Northwest. This would have meant that America would have to give up a big slice of her territory.

The British stiffened when they received news of their own military successes in America, but were a lot friendlier when they learned of British defeats. When the British peace commissioners heard of the burning of Washington they demanded that England keep all the American territory she then held. Then came news of Macdonough's great victory over the British on Lake Champlain. The Americans flatly turned down the British terms. To make it worse for the British, the Duke of Wellington, their great military idol, told them that they could hardly demand territory from the United States when they did not control the Great Lakes. But this was not all. The war against Napoleon had been costly to England in men and money. The English people were weary of war.

The result was that each side gave up its claims against the other. The treaty brought a return of peace, but did not settle a single issue over which England and the United States had gone to war. Nothing was said about impressment or the blockade. Nothing was said about the control of the Great Lakes or the Indian neutral state. What then did the treaty do aside from ending the war? It provided for the release of prisoners and the turning back of all territory conquered by either side. Since West Florida had been taken by Jackson from the Spaniards, it remained in American hands.

The treaty also provided for the naming of a commission to settle the northeastern boundary dispute between the United States and Canada. It left the questions of the Great Lakes and the right of Americans to fish off the Grand Banks to future discussions.

News of the signing of the treaty reached New York on February 11, 1815, three days after the Battle of New Orleans. Bells rang in every church spire. Lighted candles appeared in the windows of every home, and people cheered in the streets: "A peace, a peace!" In Washington the Senate quickly approved the treaty.

The Treaty of Ghent began a new era between the two nations. In 1817, England and the United States agreed to limit naval vessels on the Great Lakes to small ships. Land fortifications were not abandoned at once, but for almost a hundred years the boundary between Canada and the United States has remained unfortified. Canada and the United States have given the world a wonderful example of how to behave as good neighbors. True, England and the United States have disagreed on occasion, but the peace that was made at Ghent has lasted. It has been cemented by a close partnership between Canada and the United States in the defense of the Western Hemisphere, and in such wonderful achievements as the St. Lawrence Seaway. From being enemies, England and the United States became firm friends and allies in two world wars.

The English-speaking peoples are now closer together than they have ever been in history. There are too many dangers ahead in the world of tomorrow for the two great nations to permit themselves to drift apart.

DAWN OF A NEW ERA

On February 26, 1819, a ball was given in Washington in honor of the British minister, Charles Bagot, who was about to return to England. The Chief Justice, members of the cabinet, and other Washington notables attended. The tables were decorated with the flags of the two united countries. Upon toasting the health of the departing British minister, the band to his surprise and pleasure struck up "God Save the King," and everybody rose. The British minister than signaled to the band to play "Yankee Doodle."

A new era, an era of peace and friendship between the two great English-speaking nations, had begun.

INDEX

Adams, John, 58
Adams, John Quincy, 58
American coast, blockade of, 35-36, 44, 59
Armstrong, John, 29, 41, 49, 50
Austerlitz, Battle of, 7

Bagot, Charles, 61
Bainbridge, William, 32
Baltimore, 50
Barney, Joshua, 49
Berlin Decree (*1806*), 15
Blockade of U.S. coast, 35-36, 44, 59
Blockades of Britain and European Continent, 7-8, 15
British navy, 23, 32
Brock, Isaac, 26, 27, 28
Broke, P. B. V., 36
Brown, Jacob, 39, 45
Buffalo, 44
Burr, Aaron, 41

Calhoun, John C., 18
Canadian-U.S. boundaries, 60
Castlereagh, Lord, 58
Champlain, Lake, Battle of, 45-46, 56, 59
Cherokees, 54
Chesapeake, U.S. frigate, 2, 12, 36
Chesapeake Bay, British forces in, 48-51
Cheves, Langdon, 18
Chippewa, Battle of, 45
Clay, Henry, 17, 23, 58
Clinton, DeWitt, 34
Cochrane, Sir Alexander, 48
Cockburn, Sir George, 35
Constitution, U.S. frigate, 29, 32-33
Creeks, 51, 54

Dearborn, Fort, 27
Dearborn, Henry, 28, 38, 39
De Cadore, Duc, 16
Decatur, Stephen, 32
Declaration of war, 22
Detroit: fall of, 26
  recapture of, 41
Detroit campaign, 38, 39

Embargo Act (*1807*), 12, 14
England, French blockade of, 7-8, 15
Erie, Fort, 45
Erie, Lake, Battle of, 39-40, 56, 58
Erskine, David M., 15
European continent, British blockade of, 7-8
Eustis, William, 29

Fallen Timbers, Battle of, 17
French Revolution, 3
Frolic, H.M.S., 32

Gallatin, Albert, 58
George, Fort, 39
Ghent, Treaty of, 58-60
Great Lakes, 59, 60
Grundy, Felix, 17
Guerrière, H.M. frigate, 16, 29, 32

Hampton, Wade, 44
Harrison, William Henry, 19, 38, 40-41, 54
Hartford Convention, 34-35
Holmes, Oliver Wendell, 33
Hornet, U.S.S., 33
Horseshoe Bend, Battle of, 54
Hull, Isaac, 29, 32
Hull, William, 26, 27, 39

62

Hunters of Kentucky, The, 55-56

Indian Confederacy, 19, 41, 51
Indian tribes, 17, 19, 26, 41, 51, 54-55
Impressment of American seamen, 3-4, 8-9, 59

Jackson, Andrew, 1, 2, 22, 54, 55, 56, 59
Jackson, Francis James, 15
Java, H.M. frigate, 32
Jay, John, 4
Jay's Treaty, 4
Jefferson, Thomas, 5, 9, 12, 14, 15, 23
Johnson, Richard M., 40, 41
Jones, Jacob, 32

Key, Francis Scott, 2, 51

Lalawethika, 19, 22
Lawrence, James, 2, 33, 36
Lawrence, U.S.S., 2, 40
Leopard, H.M. frigate, 12
Little Belt, H.M. corvette, 16
London, Treaty of (Jay's Treaty), 4
Louisiana purchase, 5
Lowndes, William, 18
Lundy's Lane, Battle of, 45

Macdonough, Thomas, 46, 59
Macedonian, H.M. frigate, 32
McHenry, Fort, 2, 50-51
Macon, Nathaniel, 16
Macon's Bill No. 2, 16
Madison, James, 15, 16, 17, 22, 23, 29, 34, 49, 50, 58
Malden, Fort, 26, 40, 41
Merchant Ships, armed, 35
Michilimackinac Island, 27
Mims, Fort, 51
Monroe, James, 50
Montreal campaign, 41, 44

Napoleon Bonaparte, 1, 4-5, 7, 15, 16, 17, 23, 24, 44, 58
Napoleonic wars, 6-8, 58, 59
Nelson, Horatio, Lord, 7
New England's opposition to war, 1, 23, 33-35
New Orleans, Battle of, 1, 2, 55-56, 60
Niagara, Fort, 44
Niagara, U.S.S., 2, 40
Nicholas I, Czar, 58
Nicholson, Joseph Hopper, 51
Non-Intercourse Act (*1809*), 14, 16

"Old Ironsides," 33
Ontario campaign, 38-39
Orders in Council, 7, 15, 18, 22

Pakenham, Sir Edward, 55-56
Peacock, H.M. frigate, 33
Perry, Oliver Hazard, 2, 39-40
Pickering, Timothy, 14
Pike, Zebulon, 38
Plattsburg, 28, 45-46
Poictiers, H.M.S., 32
Porter, Peter B., 18
President, U.S. frigate, 16-17
Prevost, Sir George, 39, 45, 46

Queenston, 28

"Red Sticks," 51
Riall, General, 45
Rodgers, John, 16
Ross, Robert, 48, 50

Scott, Winfield, 38, 45
Shannon, H.M. frigate, 36
Shawnees, 17
Smith, Samuel, 50
Smyth, Alexander, 27-28
Star-Spangled Banner, The, 2, 51
Stricker, John, 50

63

Tecumseh, Chief, 17, 19, 22, 41, 51
Thames River, Battle of, 41
Tippecanoe Creek, Battle of, 19
Trafalgar, Battle of, 7

United States, U.S. frigate, 32
United States army, 23, 56
United States navy, 23, 32

Van Rensselaer, Stephen, 27-28

War hawks, 17-18, 23

Washington, George, 3, 4
Washington, D.C., 15;
   burning of, 49, 59
Wasp, U.S.S., 32
Wayne, Anthony, 17
Wellington, Duke of, 44, 59
West Florida, 59
Wilkinson, James, 41, 44, 45
Winder, William H., 49

York (Toronto), raid of, 38

4-6

3 2005 0544334 5

J 973.5 M

4-6

Morris
    First book of the War of 1812

Date Due

DISCARDED FROM THE
PORTVILLE FREE LIBRARY

PORTVILLE FREE LIBRARY
PORTVILLE, N. Y.

Member Of
Chautauqua-Cattaraugus Library System

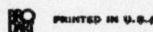